The
Lectin-Free
Cookbook

Easy and Fast Lectin-Free Recipes for Your Instant Pot Electric Pressure Cooker

by Virginia Campbell

The Lectin-Free Cookbook: Easy and Fast Lectin-Free Recipes for Your Instant Pot Electric Pressure Cooker

ISBN: 978-1-7320679-2-9

The
Lectin-Free
Cookbook

Want to help us spread the word about the lectin-free lifestyle?

Leave a review on Amazon!

A review is the best way to help spread the word about lectin-free living, and hopefully it will help the next person find their way to healthier, easier Lectin-Free Instant Pot meals, too!

To leave a review:

Google search "lectin free cookbook Virginia Campbell" and click the first Amazon link. Or, copy this URL into your browser: http://bit.ly/lectinreview.

This should take you to the Amazon book page, where you can leave a review.

Thank you so much!

The Lectin-Free Cookbook: Easy and Fast Lectin-Free Recipes for Your Instant Pot Electric Pressure Cooker

Table of Contents

Lectin-Free Instant Pot Chicken Recipes

Lectin-Free Instant Pot Seafood Recipes

Lectin-Free Instant Pot Pork Recipes

Lectin-Free Instant Pot Recipes by Category

Sometimes what I need most on busy nights is **the right recipe at the right time**. Maybe you, too? Here are all the Lectin-Free Instant Pot recipes in this book, grouped by their category, so that you can find a 20 minute recipe for when everyone's hangry, a 7 ingredient recipe for when you haven't had time to grocery shop, and a kid-friendly recipe for those cranky nights.

I hope you find that the Instant Pot electric pressure cooker is just what you need to make your new lectin-free lifestyle easy, fun, and delicious!

Kid-Friendly Recipes

7 Ingredients or Less Recipes

20 Minutes or Less Recipes

Introduction

I've never thought of myself as a dieter. (Says the woman writing a book on going lectin-free—ha!)

But then I had a daughter and life started to get even busier. Soon I realized my jeans were a little tighter and my motivation a little lower each day. Just as bad, I felt SO tired all the time. It was difficult enough to get through my to-do list each day and take care of my family, and I just couldn't seem to find the time or energy to go to the gym.

Feeling depressed that my health was always being pushed to the backburner, I finally caved and bought *The Plant Paradox: The Hidden Dangers in "Healthy" Foods That Cause Disease and Weight Gain* by Dr. Steven Gundry.

I'd first heard about lectins from a few close friends who were all going lectin-free together. They couldn't stop raving about how much better they felt. And when I realized that my friends—who were just as busy and stretched thin as I was—were suddenly healthier, thinner, and more energetic than I'd seen them in years, I realized that I needed to do whatever they were doing, and quick.

My husband and I decided to try avoiding lectins in our diet using the plan in *The Plant Paradox*. **It totally changed us**. We started thinking about food differently, and we couldn't believe how good eating lectin-free made us feel. We felt younger, stronger, and happier than we had in years.

But after the initial phases of the Plant Paradox Program, we started missing our favorite foods, like chili and sloppy joes. We needed more variety in our diet, but we didn't want to go back to our old ways, which left us feeling bloated and exhausted after dinner.

We also loved that we were cooking and eating together as a family more, and my daughter was already less stressed and more interested in what was going on in the kitchen. But we needed quicker and easier recipes and definitely more variety than the recipes included in *The Plant Paradox*. And on top of that, we needed them to be kid-friendly *and* lectin-free. Sounds like a tall order, right?

Around that time, I received an Instant Pot electric pressure cooker as a gift from my mom, who is an incredible cook and is obsessed with her Instant Pot. **That was a big breakthrough for us as a family:** the Instant Pot allowed us to finally open up our diet and start reintroducing foods like tomatoes and beans, all while spending less time in the kitchen and *still* steadily losing weight. It was a win-win-win for us!

Now, dinner at my house looks like this: I toss a few ingredients in the Instant Pot, set it to electric pressure cooking mode, then hang out in the living room, catching up with my husband or helping the kids with their homework. No more watching and stirring over the stove or peeking and prodding in the oven! And since I know the electric pressure cooker is going to destroy the toxic lectins in ingredients, I can finally feel safe eating tomatoes and other lectin-heavy ingredients on occasion again.

I hope you enjoy this collection of lectin-free Instant Pot recipes as much as my family has. My wish is that this book makes you and your family healthier and happier, one meal at a time.

If you do find these lectin-free Instant Pot recipes helpful, would you consider leaving a review on Amazon? It would mean so much to me and will hopefully help the next person find their way to an easier, healthier time in the kitchen! (To leave a review, type this URL into your browser: http://bit.ly/lectinreview).

Thank you so much for purchasing this book, and happy cooking!

Virginia

About the Lectin-Free Instant Pot Recipes in this Book

The lectin-free recipes in this book are designed with real families in mind: the kind who want to eat whole, real food, but also need to keep dinner quick, easy, and affordable.

Within these pages you'll find my very favorite lectin-free Instant Pot recipes. You can also make these recipes using another brand of electric pressure cooker, but please note that settings and cooking times may vary, so consult the manual for your particular electric pressure cooker.

These lectin-free Instant Pot recipes are the keepers that I turn to again and again, and here's why I think you'll love them, too:

Each Lectin-Free Instant Pot recipe aims for:

- **Easy-to-find, affordable ingredients:** You won't find any expensive or unpronounceable ingredients here. While there are a few keys items you'll want to buy when you first stock your lectin-free compliant pantry, I make sure they get used over and over in other recipes, so you're not stuck with an ingredient you'll never use again. (I hate that!)

- **Kid-friendly, adaptable recipes:** My kids are super picky eaters, so I always create recipes with them in mind. These lectin-free Instant Pot recipes are as simple as they can be while still being flavorful. Even better, each recipe says whether it's especially kid-friendly, and where possible, I included suggestions for how to adapt the recipe for both adult and kid taste buds.

  Remember, these recipes are designed to serve as templates for everything that's possible with your Instant Pot, so never hesitate to skip or substitute flavoring ingredients like spices or sauces if your kiddos don't like them!

- **7 Ingredient or Less recipes:** If you're like me and don't want to spend tons of time pulling ingredients from cabinets and measuring them, these lectin-free Instant Pot recipes are for you! The recipes will point out if it's a 7 Ingredient or Less recipe (not including salt and pepper, of course). That way, you can easily turn to those recipes on nights when you really want to keep things simple. (Helloooo, Wednesday night soccer practice.)

- **20 Minutes or Less recipes:** The beauty of the Instant Pot electric pressure cooker is that it's hands-free cooking, and it's incredibly fast. I've highlighted the recipes that are 20 Minutes or Less to cook once at pressure, so you can quickly turn to those when you have cranky kids or a hangry husband to feed. (Basically every night in my house…)

3 Hacks for Better Instant Pot Cooking

After experimenting with the Instant Pot electric pressure cooker for nearly a year, I've learned a few hacks that make the best use of this handy new appliance. I use these almost every single time I make a lectin-free Instant Pot recipe, and they've saved me hundreds of hours in the kitchen, plus resulted in more flavorful meals.

1. Thicken the sauce, if you have the time.

Because the Instant Pot always needs to have about 1 cup of liquid in it for the food to steam correctly, you'll get delicious broths and sauces with nearly every meal.

But sometimes, you might find that you have too much liquid after cooking, and that it's a bit thin. Sauté setting: to the rescue! If I have time, I'll often remove the food from the Instant Pot, leaving the sauce, and then set the pot on high heat on the Sauté setting. You can let it cook down as much as you want, or add a thickener to make it more like a gravy. A great lectin-free thickener is arrowroot powder. I love Starwest Botanicals brand Organic Arrowroot Powder, which you can find at specialty food stores or online at this link: http://bit.ly/starwestarrowroot.

> **To make an arrowroot powder thickener:**
> Combine 1 teaspoon arrowroot powder + 1 tablespoon water, broth, or sauce.
> Slowly whisk into the liquid and allow to cook until thickened.

2. Use the pocket of time during pressure cooking to make a side.

When I first start looking for Instant Pot recipes, it seemed like many of them had you first cook the protein, then empty the pot and cook a vegetable side. Yikes—I don't have time for that! If you don't either, here's what I suggest: get your Instant Pot recipe locked and loaded, then use the time during pressure cooking to toss together quick roasted lectin-free vegetables, spiralizer some carrots, or microwave a few baked sweet potatoes.

My favorite lectin-free vegetable side is a big tray of brussels sprouts, cauliflower, or broccoli, which I cook under the broiler instead of roasting, to save even more time.

> **To make quick and easy broiled vegetables:**
> Toss 1-inch pieces of any oven-friendly veg with olive oil, salt, and pepper.
> Place under the broiler until crispy, watching carefully so they don't burn.

3. Taste your food before serving and add more salt and pepper, if necessary.

We all like our food at different levels of saltiness and pepperiness, so please always take my measurements as a suggestion, not a rule! This is especially true of Instant Pot recipes, since you're often using broth as the steaming liquid. Different brands of broth have vastly different salt content, so if you're unsure how salty your broth might be, use less salt before pressure cooking. You can always add more salt and pepper once you open up the pot again!

Chapter 1: An Overview of the Lectin-Free Diet

Lectins are highly toxic proteins found in certain foods like beans, grains, vegetables, fruit, conventional dairy, and others. These proteins cause widespread inflammation in the body, leading to weight gain, brain fog, and a whole host of digestive issues and diseases.

The lectin-free diet is an elimination diet, meaning that it's designed to cut out foods that have high amounts of lectins and which cause inflammation or food sensitivities in many people.

Oftentimes, we *think* we have no problem eating certain foods, but we're usually too busy, too distracted, or too out-of-tune with our bodies to notice that they're making us feel bloated, tired, or just heavy-feeling. Yet, year after year, we gain weight and can't seem to pinpoint why.

But by seeing how we feel when we cut those foods from our diets, we can finally—usually for the first time in our lives—see how our bodies feel when we fill them only with real, nourishing food.

Since this is a cookbook and not a diet book (and I'm a mom and cook and not a doctor!), I won't get into the science of the lectin free diet and why it works. But if you haven't already, I highly advise you to buy *The Plant Paradox: The Hidden Dangers in "Healthy" Foods That Cause Disease and Weight Gain* by Dr. Steven Gundry for a full exploration of the science behind the lectin-free diet.

You can also find a full and complete list of the "yes" foods and the "no" foods for a lectin-free diet online at **www.gundrymd.com/plant-paradox-shopping-list**. Or use the quick recap below to quickly see what to eat and what not to eat when going lectin-free:

What Not to Eat on a Lectin-Free Diet

Grains

No pasta, bread, rice, corn, quinoa, barley, farro, wheat, and other grains.

Legumes

No beans, peas, lentils, chickpeas, peanuts, soy in any form, and other legumes.

(**Note:** In later phases of a lectin-free diet, you can have legumes if they're pressure cooked, which greatly reduces the amount of lectins in them. For that reason, we've included several recipes in this book for pressure cooking beans, but please use your own judgment and listen to your body if you have trouble digesting beans.)

Dairy products

No conventional milk, cheese, yogurt, cream, butter and other dairy.

(**Note:** Ghee, also called clarified butter, is allowed, as are dairy products made from goat or sheep milk, certain high-fat cheeses, and several other exceptions. Since it was our goal to keep these recipes simple and easy, we've designed them so that they don't rely on dairy—only ghee and extra virgin olive oil!)

Sugar

No sugar, maple syrup, agave, and others. Stevia and certain other sweeteners are okay.

Certain fruits and vegetables

No tomatoes (unless peeled and deseeded), cucumbers (unless peeled and deseeded), bell peppers (unless peeled and deseeded), zucchini, squash, peas, eggplant, ripe bananas, melons, pumpkins, and all fruit unless it's in season.

To read more about the lectin free diet, I highly recommend these two books:

The Plant Paradox: The Hidden Dangers in "Healthy" Foods That Cause Weight Gain and Disease by Dr. Steven R. Gundry

Use this link if you'd like to check out *The Plant Paradox*:
http://bit.ly/theplantparadox.

The Plant Paradox Cookbook: 100 Delicious Recipes to Help You Lose Weight, Heal Your Gut, and Live Lectin-Free by Dr. Steven R. Gundry

Use this link if you'd like to check out *The Plant Paradox Cookbook*:
http://bit.ly/plantparadoxcookbook.

What to Eat on a Lectin-Free Diet

The great news is that there are so many foods you CAN eat that are lectin-free friendly, and once you start adjusting to this new way of eating and seeing how amazing it makes you feel, you won't want to go back to your carb-loading, sweet tooth ways.

You can eat as much as you want of these lectin-free foods:

Lectin-Free Compliant Foods:
> Meat, grass-fed
> Poultry, pastured
> Seafood, wild-caught
> Vegetables, except for those on the "no" list
> Sweet potatoes
> Nuts and seeds, excluding peanuts, pumpkin seeds, sunflower, chia, and cashews
> Olive oil, ghee, and European butter
> Stevia, monk fruit, and certain other natural sweeteners
> Ice cream, if dairy-free and with less than 1g sugar
> Dark chocolate, if at least 72% cacao

The following are popular Lectin-Free ingredients:
> Almond flour
> Almond milk
> Arrowroot Powder
> Bacon
> Cacao
> Olive Oil
> Carob
> Coconut Flour
> Coconut Water
> Coconut Aminos
> Coffee
> Dates
> Dark chocolate
> Ghee (clarified butter)
> Hemp Seeds
> Pecans
> Pistachios
> Mustard
> Stevia
> Tahini
> Walnuts

Sanity-Saving Substitutions and Your Lectin-Free Pantry

While it may seem like many of your favorite foods are lectin-packed, once you get the hang of the substitutions, you'll see that you can still cook and enjoy many of your favorite recipes. With the right items in your lectin-free pantry, you'll quickly and easily be able to adapt your cooking to your healthy new life.

Instead of wheat flour, **use almond flour**.
> Use a quality brand like Bob's Red Mill Almond Flour, available online here: http://bit.ly/redmillalmondflour.

Instead of soy sauce, **use coconut aminos.**
> The Coconut Secret brand, which can be found at http://bit.ly/coconutsecretaminos, is lectin-free.

Instead of regular mayonnaise, **use Duke's Mayonnaise.**
> You can find it online at http://bit.ly/dukesmayonaise or at select supermarkets. It's the only brand without added sugar.

Instead of butter, **use ghee (also known as clarified butter).**
> I swear by the Trader Joe's brand, which you can also buy on Amazon at http://bit.ly/traderjoesghee.

Instead of regular barbeque sauce, **use Not Ketchup BBQ Sauce.**
> You can find it on Amazon at http://bit.ly/notketchupbbqsauce; it's one of the few lectin-free, tomato-free BBQ sauces.

Instead of milk, use **unsweetened original almond milk or unsweetened coconut milk.**
> Pacific is a popular almond milk brand and can be used in savory dishes. It can be found online here: http://bit.ly/pacificfoodsalmondmilk.
>
> Unsweetened coconut milk is best used in Indian or Asian dishes due to its coconut flavor. Thai Kitchen is a popular lectin-free brand and is available online at http://bit.ly/thaikitchencoconutmilk.

Instead of sugar, use stevia.
> Stevia is easily found at most supermarkets these days and online at http://bit.ly/pyurestevia, and you can buy it in powder or liquid form.

Instead of cornstarch for thickening, use arrowroot powder.
> You can find it online at http://bit.ly/starwestarrowroot, and even though it can be a bit pricey, it lasts forever.

An important note on broth:

Because of how the Instant Pot pressure cooks, it typically requires about 1 cup of liquid in the pot. You'll see that many of the recipes in this book call for chicken, beef, or vegetable broth, but please keep in mind that the quality of your broth will heavily influence the flavor of the final dish.

Try Bone Broth by Kettle & Fire, available here: http://bit.ly/kettlefirebeefbonebroth, for a top-of-the-line, just-like-homemade flavor.

Or for a more affordable, yet still delicious, option, try Pacific's organic, free-range line, available at many grocery stores or online at http://bit.ly/pacificchickenbroth.

Chapter 2: Understanding the Instant Pot Electric Pressure Cooker

The Instant Pot is America's #1 bestselling electric pressure cooker for a reason: it's so much more than a pressure cooker! The Instant Pot is a first-of-its kind multi-cooker, which combines a slow cooker, pressure cooker, and rice cooker into one handy electric appliance. Even better, the Instant Pot has a sauté function which allows you to brown vegetables, sear meat, and easily build flavor right in the pot, unlike traditional slow cookers or pressure cookers.

Which Instant Pot model is right for you?

All of the Instant Pot models will have the basic buttons and functions you need to make every recipe in this book. However, there's a lot of variation from model to model, so here are a few tips for finding the Instant Pot electric pressure cooker that's right for you:

If you want all 9 settings:
> Get the Instant Pot DUO Plus 60 6 Quart 9-in-1 model here: http://bit.ly/instantpot9in1

If you cook for a crowd:
> Get the Instant Pot DUO80 7-in-1 in the 8 quart size here: http://bit.ly/instantpoteightqt

If you have a small kitchen:
> Get the Instant Pot DUO80 7-in1 in the 3 quart size here: http://bit.ly/instantpot3qt.

If you're on a budget:
> Get the Instant Pot LUX60 V3 6-in-1 in the 6 quart size here: http://bit.ly/instantpot6qt

Which Instant Pot accessories are helpful?

While you don't need additional accessories to make any of the recipes in this book, you might find it helpful to have a few Instant Pot-friendly items to make things a little easier on yourself.

For steaming vegetables, seafood, or delicate cuts of meat:
> Instant Pot makes **a silicone steamer set,** available here, http://bit.ly/instantpotsteamerset, which makes it easier to use the Steam setting.

For easily removing the trivet or pot without burning yourself:
> Try Instant Pot's **silicone mini mitts**, which are practical, easy to store, and cute to boot! They can be found online here: http://bit.ly/instantpotminimitts

For storing leftovers in your pot in the refrigerator:
> You can get a **silicone lid cover** here: http://bit.ly/instantpotsiliconelid. It fits snugly over your pot, saving you clean-up time after dinner.

For doubling up on your pressure cooking:

Get **an Instant Pot-approved back-up pot**, for those times when you want to cook recipes back-to-back in your pot without doing dishes in between. Available online at http://bit.ly/instantpotinnerpot.

For more Instant Pot recipes:

I love *The Essential Instant Pot Cookbook* by Coco Morante and *Dinner in an Instant* by Melissa Clark. Not all the recipes are lectin-free, but you'll find great inspiration and you can modify many of the recipes to fit your new lectin-free lifestyle.

Get *The Essential Instant Pot Cookbook* here: http://bit.ly/essentialinstantpot
Get *Dinner in an Instant* here: http://bit.ly/dinnerinstant

How does the Instant Pot pressure cook?

You may be coming to the Instant Pot with preconceived notions of what a pressure cooker is. Maybe you've heard stories that they can overflow or spray food everywhere, or maybe you remember the old-fashioned pressure cookers that loudly (and annoyingly) whistled.

Forget all those ideas, because the Instant Pot is different. Because the Instant Pot is an *electric* pressure cooker that was specifically designed to be safer than stovetop pressure cookers, it has few of the issues of old-fashioned pressure cookers. But if you're like me and like to know how things work, you might be wondering how, exactly, the Instant Pot cooks food using the pressure cooking setting.

The Instant Pot electric pressure cooker program begins when you set the Pressure Release valve to "Sealing." From there, you select the program and set the desired time. The Instant Pot will give you 30-60 seconds to make your selections, then it will automatically initiate the program.

As the Instant Pot begins to build heat, the pressure increases in the pot and the boiling point of the water or liquid in the pot also increases. As more and more steam is generated, the pressure continues to increase inside the pot. The water begins to reach a very high temperature, yet the high pressure and the increased boiling point prevents the water from boiling or evaporating.

The high-heat, high-moisture environment of the Instant Pot means you get exceptionally quick cooking times and incredibly moist food. Even typically dry cuts of meat, such as boneless skinless chicken breasts come out juicy and moist in just a few minutes. This makes it almost impossible to overcook or dry out your food—and who doesn't want that?!

Inside Your Instant Pot Pressure Cooker

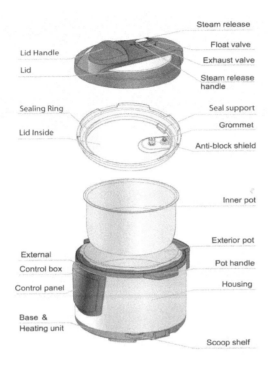

While other electric pressure cookers may have features that are different from the Instant Pot, almost all electric pressure cookers have several key parts:

Inner pot. Sometimes also referred to as the cooking pot. The inner pot is stainless steel, so it's easy to wash and can also be used to store leftovers in the refrigerator.

Heating element. The heating element is electric, meaning that you can plug in the pot and set it on your countertop, just like a slow cooker. This makes it perfect for small kitchens!

Sensors. The Instant Pot has several built-in pressure and temperature sensors that make it safer than a nonelectric pressure cooker. These sensors monitor the internal environment, maintain the desired cooking conditions, and help protect you from possible mishaps.

Locking mechanism. The Instant Pot has a sealing ring that creates a completely airtight chamber inside the pot so that steam can build up. Once you turn the pot lid to the Closed position, the vacuum seal is formed. The lid locks in place, so that you can't accidentally open the lid when the pot is at a high pressure.

Push down pressure release: The valves that are installed in the Instant Pot are designed with an innovative Anti-Block Shield that allows them to automatically react to changing conditions in the pot. The valves remain locked until the pressure goes beyond the specified threshold, at which point the valve pushes itself upward, slowly releasing the pressure and returning it to normal levels. These release valves are intelligently controlled with electronic sensors which automatically alter the settings depending on the type of food you're cooking.

Understanding the Instant Pot Buttons

The Instant Pot is preprogrammed with various cooking settings, so that you can quickly and easily select the cooking program that's right for each kind of food. The Instant Pot company has spent years assimilating data from hundreds of chefs all over the world to arrive at these pre-programmed times, so the settings have a high level of accuracy.

Of course, a setting like "Bean" will only work if you have the recommended quantity of beans and liquid in the pot, so it's important to follow an Instant Pot recipe rather than just guess at the setting. You can also find comprehensive cooking times for basic ingredients in the Cooking Times for the Instant Pot Electric Pressure Cooker chart at the back of this book.

The Instant Pot comes in many models and sizes, so you may not have these exact buttons. If not, don't worry: you can always use the Manual or Pressure Cook setting to replicate the same results produced by the other buttons.

Sauté: Use this to sauté vegetables, sear meat, simmer a soup, thicken a sauce, or otherwise cook food over high heat like you would on the stovetop. This setting should only be used with the lid removed. Many Instant Pot models include buttons that allow you to adjust the heat to Low, Normal, or High, just as you would on the stovetop.

Keep Warm/Cancel: Use this button to turn your pressure cooker off or reset the cooking program. You can also use it to keep food warm in the Instant Pot until you're ready to serve it.

Manual: This is your go-to button for setting a cooking program. The manual button lets you set any cooking time at any pressure level, so it's a good back-up if your Instant Pot doesn't have a specific program called for in a recipe.

Soup: This will set the program to pressure cook, and you can adjust the time to 30 minutes of cooking time (at normal); 40 minutes (at more); 20 minutes (at less).

Meat/Stew: This will set the program to pressure cook, and you can adjust the time to 35 minutes of cooking time (at normal); 45 minutes (at more); 20 minutes (at less).

Bean/Chili: This will set the program to pressure cook, and you can adjust the time to 30 minutes of cooking time (at normal); 40 minutes (at more); 25 minutes (at less)

Poultry: This will set the program to pressure cook, and you can adjust the time to 15 minutes of cooking time (at normal); 30 minutes (at more); 5 minutes (at less).

Rice: This is a fully automated mode which allows you to easily cook rice on low pressure. It will adjust the timer automatically, depending on the amount of water and rice present inside the inner cooking pot.

Multi-Grain: This will set the program to pressure cook, and you can adjust the time to 40 minutes of cooking time (at normal); 45 minutes (at more); 20 minutes (at less).

Porridge: This will set the program to pressure cook, and you can adjust the time to 20 minutes of cooking time (at normal); 30 minutes (at more); 15 minutes (at less)

Steam: This setting is useful for quickly steaming vegetables, seafood, or thin cuts of meats. It will set your pressure cooker to high pressure with 10 minutes of cooking time (at normal); 15 minutes (at more; 3 minutes (at less). Use this setting with a steamer basket or trivet for best results, so that your food is elevated from the 1 cup of liquid that will also be in the pot.

Slow Cooker: This button will initiate the slow cooker function and set it for a 4-hour cook time. However, you can change the temperature—low will be at 190-201 degrees Fahrenheit; normal is 194-205 degrees Fahrenheit; high is199-210 degrees Fahrenheit.

Pressure: This button allows you to switch between high and low-pressure settings.

Yogurt: This is an automatic setting that allows you to make yogurt in individual servings. Make sure you find a trustworthy, tested recipe for making yogurt using this function.

Timer: This button allows you to adjust the cooking time by pressing the + or – buttons.

Lectin-Free Instant Pot Egg Recipes

Foolproof Hard-Boiled and Soft-Boiled Eggs

Kid-Friendly
20 Minutes or Less
7 Ingredients or Less

Makes 2-12
Prep Time: 1 minute
Cook Time: 3-5 minutes

Ingredients
2-12 eggs (You can cook as many as fit in one layer in the pot, but remember that they should be pastured or omega3 eggs to be lectin-free diet friendly.)

Directions
Place the Instant Pot trivet inside the pot. Arrange eggs in one layer on top of the trivet and add 1 cup of water to the pot.

Lock the lid and set the Pressure Release to Sealing. Select the Pressure Cook or Manual setting and set the cooking time to 5 minutes for hard-boiled eggs or 3 minutes for soft-boiled eggs at high pressure.

Once the timer goes off, use a kitchen towel or oven mitts to protect your hand and move the Pressure Release knob to Venting to perform a quick pressure release.

Cool eggs under running water and peel.

Ham and Broccoli Crustless Quiche

Kid-Friendly
7 Ingredients or Less

Serves 4
Prep Time: 10 minutes
Cook Time: 30 minutes

Ingredients
6 eggs, pastured or omega 3
2 teaspoons of ghee, divided
½ cup diced ham
½ cup broccoli florets, chopped small
1 green onion, chopped
¼ teaspoon salt
Pepper to taste

Directions
Place the trivet in the bottom of the Instant Pot and add 1 cup of water to the pot. Grease a 1 quart round oven-safe dish (such as a casserole or soufflé dish) with 1 teaspoon of ghee.

In a medium bowl, beat the eggs and add the remaining 1 teaspoon of ghee, ham, broccoli, green onion, salt, and pepper. Stir well, then pour into the prepared dish.

Loosely cover the dish with aluminum foil and place inside the Instant Pot on top of the trivet. (Use an aluminum foil sling to lift in and out of the pot, if necessary.)

Lock the lid and set the Pressure Release to Sealing. Select the Pressure Cook or Manual setting and set the cooking time to 30 minutes at high pressure.

Once the timer goes off, let sit for at least 10 minutes; the pressure will release naturally. Then switch the Pressure Release to Venting to allow any last steam out.

Carefully remove the dish from the Instant Pot and serve warm.

Note: You can also use this recipe as a template for substituting any omelet or quiche ingredients you most like.

Lectin-Free Instant Pot Soup and Stew Recipes

Creamy Cauliflower and Sage Soup

Kid-Friendly
7 Ingredients or Less
20 Minutes or Less

Serves 4
Prep Time: 10 minutes
Cook Time: 10 minutes

Ingredients
1 teaspoon olive oil
1 onion, chopped
4 cloves garlic, minced
1 tablespoon fresh sage, or 1 teaspoon ground sage
8 cups cauliflower florets
3 cups chicken broth
½ teaspoon salt
Pepper to taste
½ cup unsweetened coconut milk

Directions
Select the Sauté setting and heat the olive oil. Add the onion and cook until translucent, about 3-5 minutes. Add the garlic and sage and cook for 1 minute. Add the cauliflower, chicken broth, salt, and pepper, and stir well.

Press Cancel to reset the cooking method. Lock the lid and set the Pressure Release to Sealing. Select the Pressure Cook or Manual setting and set the cooking time to 10 minutes at high pressure.

Once the timer goes off, let sit for at least 10 minutes; the pressure will release naturally. Then switch the Pressure Release to Venting to allow any last steam out.

Open the Instant Pot and puree the soup using an immersion blender or by transferring it to a stand blender. Stir in the unsweetened coconut milk and add salt and pepper to taste.

Luscious and Light Carrot Soup

20 Minutes or Less

Serves 4
Prep Time: 10 minutes
Cook Time: 15 minutes

Ingredients
1 tablespoon ghee
½ yellow onion, chopped
3 cloves garlic, minced
1 tablespoon curry powder
1 teaspoon cayenne pepper (optional)
1½ cups vegetable broth
8-10 large carrots, peeled and chopped
1 14-oz can unsweetened coconut milk

Directions
Select the Sauté setting on the Instant Pot and heat the ghee. Add the onion and garlic and cook, stirring often, until the onion is translucent, 3-5 minutes. Add remaining ingredients, except coconut milk, and stir well.

Press Cancel to reset the cooking method. Lock the lid and set the Pressure Release to Sealing. Select the Pressure Cook or Manual setting and set the cooking time to 15 minutes at high pressure.

Once the timer goes off, let sit for at least 10 minutes; the pressure will release naturally. Then switch the Pressure Release to Venting to allow any last steam out.

Open the Instant Pot and puree the soup using an immersion blender or by transferring it to a stand blender. Stir in the unsweetened coconut milk and add salt and pepper to taste.

My Signature Lemon Chicken Soup

Kid-Friendly

Serves 4
Prep Time: 10 minutes
Cook Time: 6 minutes

Ingredients
2 tablespoons ghee
1 onion, chopped
3 cloves garlic, minced
2 medium carrots, peeled and sliced
3 stalks celery, sliced
8 cups chicken broth
8 oz. mushrooms, sliced
1 tablespoon fresh thyme, or 1 teaspoon dried thyme
Salt to taste
Pepper to taste
1½ lbs. boneless skinless chicken breasts or thighs
1 bunch kale, stemmed and roughly chopped
2 lemons, juiced
Optional: lemon wedges for serving

Directions
Select the Sauté setting and heat the ghee. Add the onion, garlic, carrots, and celery and sauté for 4-6 minutes. Add the chicken broth, mushrooms, and thyme. Taste and add salt and pepper to taste. Add the chicken breasts or thighs and stir well.

Press Cancel to reset the cooking method. Lock the lid and set the Pressure Release to Sealing. Select the Soup setting and set the cooking time to 6 minutes at high pressure.

Once the timer goes off, let sit for at least 10 minutes; the pressure will release naturally. Then switch the Pressure Release to Venting to allow any last steam out.

Open the Instant Pot and remove the chicken and shred. Add the chicken back to the pot and stir in the kale and lemon juice. Ladle into bowls and serve with an extra squeeze of lemon, drizzle of olive oil, or fresh cracked pepper.

Fuss-Free French Onion Soup

7 Ingredients or Less
20 Minutes or Less

Serves 4
Prep Time: 5 minutes
Cook Time: 10 minutes

Ingredients
3 tablespoons ghee
3 large onions, halved and then thinly sliced
1 tablespoon balsamic vinegar
2 tablespoons red wine vinegar
6 cups beef or pork broth
2 large sprigs fresh thyme
1 teaspoon salt

Directions
Select the Sauté setting and heat the ghee. Add the onions and stir constantly until completely cooked down and caramelized. This can take 10-20 minutes or more, depending on your onions and the heat of your Instant Pot. If the onions begin to blacken at the edges, use the Adjust button to reduce the heat to Less.

Once the onions have caramelized, add the balsamic vinegar, red wine vinegar, broth, and thyme and scrape up any browned bits from the bottom of the pot.

Press Cancel to reset the cooking method. Lock the lid and set the Pressure Release to Sealing. Select the Soup setting and set the cooking time to 10 minutes at high pressure.

Once the timer goes off, let sit for at least 10 minutes; the pressure will release naturally. Then switch the Pressure Release to Venting to allow any last steam out.

Open the Instant Pot and discard the thyme stems. Season with salt and pepper to taste.

Note: Because this soup is so simple, a good quality broth is essential. I recommend the Kettle & Fire, available at http://bit.ly/kettlefirebeefbonebroth, or Pacific brands, found here: http://bit.ly/pacificchickenbroth.

Creamy Broccoli and Leek Soup

Kid-Friendly
20 Minutes or Less

Serves 4
Prep Time: 5 minutes
Cook Time: 5 minutes

Ingredients
2 tablespoons ghee
3 medium leeks, white parts only (frozen is fine!)
2 shallots, chopped
1 large head broccoli, cut into florets
4 cups vegetable broth
1 cup unsweetened coconut milk
Pepper to taste
Salt to taste
Optional: ¼ cup walnuts, toasted
Optional: ¼ cup coconut cream

Directions
Select the Sauté setting and heat the ghee. Add the leeks and shallots and cook, stirring constantly, until softened, 4-6 minutes. Add the broccoli and sauté another 5-6 minutes. Add the vegetable broth and stir well.

Press Cancel to reset the cooking method. Lock the lid and set the Pressure Release to Sealing. Select the Pressure Cook or Manual setting and set the cooking time to 5 minutes at high pressure.

Once the timer goes off, let sit for at least 10 minutes; the pressure will release naturally. Then switch the Pressure Release to Venting to allow any last steam out.

Open the Instant Pot and puree the soup using an immersion blender or by transferring it to a stand blender. Stir in the unsweetened coconut milk and add salt and pepper to taste.

Ladle into bowls and top with toasted walnuts or a drizzle of coconut cream.

Immune-Boost Chard and Sweet Potato Stew

20 Minutes or Less

Serves 2
Prep Time: 10 minutes
Cook Time: 8 minutes

Ingredients
2 tablespoons olive oil
1 teaspoon cumin seeds, or 1 teaspoon ground cumin
1 medium onion, diced
2 medium sweet potatoes, peeled and in ½ inch cubes
½ teaspoon turmeric
1 tablespoon fresh ginger, peeled and minced
1 teaspoon salt
1 teaspoon ground coriander
2 cups vegetable broth
1 bunch Swiss chard
Optional: lemon wedges for serving

Directions
Select the Sauté setting and heat the olive oil. Add the onion and cook until translucent, 3-5 minutes. If using cumin seeds, add them now and toast them for 1-3 minutes, until fragrant. Otherwise, add the ground cumin in the next step.

Add the sweet potato, ground cumin (if using), ginger, turmeric, coriander, and salt and cook for 3-4 minutes. Add the vegetable broth and chard. Taste and add more salt and pepper if needed.

Press Cancel to reset the cooking method. Lock the lid and set the Pressure Release to Sealing. Select the Pressure Cook or Manual setting and set the cooking time to 8 minutes at high pressure.

Once the timer goes off, let sit for at least 10 minutes; the pressure will release naturally. Then switch the Pressure Release to Venting to allow any last steam out.

Ladle into bowls and serve warm with a squeeze of lemon juice, if desired.

Moroccan Lentil Soup

Kid-Friendly
20 Minutes or Less

Serves 4
Prep Time: 10 minutes
Cook Time: 10 minutes

Ingredients
1 tablespoon olive oil
1 small onion, chopped
3 cloves garlic, minced
1 lb. ground beef
1 tablespoon cumin
1 teaspoon garlic powder
1 teaspoon chili powder
1 teaspoon salt, plus more to taste
¼ teaspoon cinnamon
Pepper to taste
5 cups beef broth
2 cups green or brown lentils

Directions
Select the Sauté setting and heat the olive oil. Add the onion and garlic and sauté until fragrant, 2-3 minutes. Add the ground beef and cumin, garlic powder, chili powder, salt, cinnamon, and pepper. Cook until very well-browned and beginning to sear. Add the beef broth and scrape up any browned bits from the bottom of the pot. Add the lentils and stir well.

Press Cancel to reset the cooking method. Lock the lid and set the Pressure Release to Sealing. Select the Soup setting and set the cooking time to 10 minutes at high pressure.

Once the timer goes off, let sit for at least 10 minutes; the pressure will release naturally. Then switch the Pressure Release to Venting to allow any last steam out.

Open the Instant Pot and taste; add more salt and pepper to taste. Ladle into bowls and serve with a drizzle of olive oil or fresh cracked pepper.

Lectin-Free Instant Pot Chicken Recipes

One-Pot Thyme Chicken and Sweet Potatoes

Kid-Friendly
20 Minutes or Less

Serves 4
Prep Time: 10 minutes
Cook Time: 10 minutes

Ingredients
2 lbs. boneless skinless chicken breasts
1 teaspoon salt, divided
1 tablespoon olive oil
1 cup chicken broth
2 cloves garlic, minced
1 cup pearl onions (can be frozen), or 1 medium onion, sliced
2 cups carrots, diced
4 medium sweet potatoes, cut in 1-inch pieces
1 sprig fresh rosemary, or 1 teaspoon dried rosemary
1 sprig fresh thyme, or 1 teaspoon dried thyme
Pepper to taste

Directions
Season the chicken breasts on both sides with ½ teaspoon salt. Select the Sauté setting on the Instant Pot and heat the olive oil. Brown the chicken, about 5 minutes per side.

Add the chicken broth and scraping up any browned bits from the bottom of the pot. Layer in the garlic and onion, top with carrots, and then sweet potatoes. Sprinkle the sweet potatoes with rosemary, thyme, and the remaining ½ teaspoon of salt.

Press Cancel to reset the cooking method. Lock the lid and set the Pressure Release to Sealing. Select the Poultry setting and set the cooking time to 10 minutes.

Once the timer goes off, let sit for at least 10 minutes; the pressure will release naturally. Then switch the Pressure Release to Venting to allow any last steam out.

Open the lid, and add salt and pepper to taste. Serve in bowls with the broth.

Game-Time Buffalo Wings and Cauliflower

Kid-Friendly
20 Minutes or Less
7 Ingredients or Less

Serves 4
Prep Time: 1 minute
Cook Time: 5 minutes

Ingredients
½ cup Frank's Red Hot Sauce (Hot sauce is typically compliant because it is fermented.)
¼ cup ghee
2 lbs. chicken wings
½ head cauliflower, cut into florets

Directions

Add 1 cup of water to the Instant Pot and place the trivet in the pot. Arrange the chicken wings on top of the trivet, then arrange the cauliflower on top of the chicken wings. Be sure you can easily close the lid.

Lock the lid and set the Pressure Release to Sealing. Select the Pressure Cook or Manual setting and set the cooking time to 5 minutes at high pressure.

Meanwhile, in a small bowl, combine the hot sauce and ghee. Set aside.

Once the timer goes off, let sit for 5 minutes, then switch the Pressure Release to Venting to allow any last steam out.

Toss the wings and cauliflower in the buffalo sauce and serve warm.

Optional: For crispier, more charred wings and cauliflower, spread the wings on a baking sheet and the cauliflower on another. Set under the broiler until they reach your desired level of crispiness.

Fiesta Pulled Chicken Taco Bar

Kid-Friendly
7 Ingredients or Less
20 Minutes or Less

Serves 4
Prep Time: 5 minutes
Cook Time: 7-10 minutes

Ingredients
2 pounds of boneless skinless chicken breast or thighs
1 tablespoon chili powder
½ tablespoon ground cumin
1 teaspoon garlic powder
1 teaspoon oregano
½ teaspoon salt
1 cup chicken broth
1 head butter lettuce, separated into lettuce cups
Optional: guacamole, green onions, black olives, or any other favorite taco toppings

Directions
Season chicken on both sides with chili powder, cumin, garlic powder, oregano, and salt. Select the Sauté setting on the Instant Pot and heat the olive oil. Brown the chicken, about 5 minutes per side. Add the chicken broth and scraping up any browned bits from the bottom of the pot.

Press Cancel to reset the cooking method. Lock the lid and set the Pressure Release to Sealing. Select the Poultry setting and set the cooking time to 7 minutes for breasts and 10 minutes for thighs at high pressure.

Once the timer goes off, let sit for at least 10 minutes; the pressure will release naturally. Then switch the Pressure Release to Venting to allow any last steam out.

Open the lid and taste, adding more salt and pepper if necessary. Shred the chicken, and allow each person to assemble their own lettuce tacos.

Note: For a thicker sauce, remove 1 tablespoon of sauce to a small bowl. Dissolve 1 teaspoon arrowroot powder in the sauce, then add back to the Instant Pot and whisk well. Select the Sauté setting and allow to cook for a few minutes, whisking often, until thickened.

Chicken Marsala with Mashed Sweet Potatoes

Kid-Friendly

Serves 5
Prep Time: 10 minutes
Cook Time: 30 minutes

Ingredients
4 medium sweet potatoes, pricked all over to allow steam to vent
2 lbs. boneless skinless chicken breast
1 teaspoon salt
Pepper to taste
1 teaspoon olive oil
2 cloves garlic, minced
1/8 cup champagne vinegar or white wine vinegar
1 cup sliced mushrooms
½ cup chicken broth
Optional: 1 teaspoon arrowroot powder
Optional: fresh basil for serving

Directions
Place the trivet inside the Instant Pot, add 1 cup water, and place the sweet potatoes on the trivet. Lock the lid and set the Pressure Release to Sealing. Select the Manual or Pressure Cook setting and set the timer to 10 minutes at high pressure. Once the timer goes off, let sit for at least 10 minutes; the pressure will release naturally. Then switch the Pressure Release to Venting to allow any last steam out. Remove the sweet potatoes and set aside to cool.

Discard the water, dry the pot, and select the Sauté setting. Heat the olive oil, then add the chicken, salt, and pepper to taste. Sear the chicken until browned, about 5 minutes on each side. Add the garlic, vinegar, mushrooms, and broth, and stir to combine, scraping up any browned bits from the bottom of the pan.

Press Cancel to reset the cooking method. Lock the lid and set the Pressure Release to Sealing. Select the Poultry setting and set the cooking time to 7 minutes at high pressure.

Meanwhile, scoop the insides out of the sweet potatoes, mash, and season with salt, pepper, and ghee to taste. Once the Instant Pot timer goes off, use a kitchen towel or oven mitts to protect your hand and move the Pressure Release knob to Venting to perform a quick pressure release.

Open the lid and taste, adding more salt and pepper if necessary. Serve the chicken with the sweet potato mash and top with the marsala sauce, mushrooms, and fresh basil, if desired

Note: For a thicker sauce, remove 1 tablespoon of sauce to a small bowl. Dissolve 1 teaspoon arrowroot powder in the sauce, then add back to the Instant Pot and whisk well. Select the Sauté setting and allow to cook for a few minutes, whisking often, until thickened.

Lemon Pepper Chicken with Cauliflower Mash

Kid-Friendly
7 Ingredients or Less
20 Minutes or Less

Serves 4
Prep Time: 15 minutes
Cook Time: 15 minutes

Ingredients
3 lemons, zested and juiced
1 teaspoon garlic powder
1½ teaspoons black pepper
1 teaspoon salt
2 tablespoons ghee, divided
2 lbs. bone-in chicken thighs
1 cup chicken broth
4 cups cauliflower, in large florets

Directions

In a small bowl, combine the lemon zest, garlic powder, pepper, and salt.

Select the Sauté setting and heat 1 tablespoon of the ghee. Season the chicken thighs on both sides with the lemon pepper rub. Add the chicken thighs to the pot and brown well on each side, about 4 minutes per side. You may need to work in batches.

Add chicken broth and scrape up any browned bits from the bottom of the pot. Place the trivet on top of the chicken and layer the cauliflower florets on top of the trivet. Season cauliflower lightly with salt and pepper.

Press Cancel to reset the cooking method. Lock the lid and set the Pressure Release to Sealing. Select the Poultry setting and set the cooking time to 15 minutes at high pressure.

Once the timer goes off, use a kitchen towel or oven mitts to protect your hand and move the Pressure Release knob to Venting to perform a quick pressure release.

Open the lid, remove the cauliflower to a bowl, and mash with the remaining 1 tablespoon ghee and salt and pepper to taste. Serve the chicken with the cauliflower mash and drizzle the chicken with as much lemon juice as desired before serving.

Note: For a thicker sauce, remove 1 tablespoon of sauce to a small bowl. Dissolve 1 teaspoon arrowroot powder in the sauce, then add back to the Instant Pot and whisk well. Select the Sauté setting and allow to cook for a few minutes, whisking often, until thickened.

Cranberry and Balsamic Chicken

20 Minutes or Less

Serves 4
Prep Time: 5 minutes
Cook Time: 10 minutes

Ingredients
2 lbs. boneless skinless chicken thighs
1 tablespoon olive oil
½ teaspoon salt
Pepper to taste
½ small red onion, diced
1 cup cranberry juice (Be sure it is no sugar added, such as Knudsen Family brand, which can be purchased online at http://bit.ly/knudsencranberryjuice.)
3 tablespoons balsamic vinegar
1 tablespoon coconut aminos
½ tablespoon garlic powder
½ tablespoon dried rosemary
Optional: arrowroot powder

Directions
Select the Sauté setting and heat the olive oil. Season the thighs with salt and pepper, then brown on one side, 4-5 minutes. Flip the thighs, add the red onion, and allow both to brown for 4-5 minutes more.

Meanwhile, in a small bowl, mix the cranberry juice, balsamic vinegar, coconut aminos, garlic powder, and dried rosemary. Add to the Instant Pot and stir, scraping up any browned bits from the bottom of the pot.

Press Cancel to reset the cooking method. Lock the lid and set the Pressure Release to Sealing. Select the Poultry setting and set the cooking time to 10 minutes at high pressure.

With a kitchen towel or oven mitts protecting your hand, move the Pressure Release knob to Venting to perform a quick pressure release. Open the lid and taste, adding more salt and pepper if necessary. Remove the chicken, transfer to a platter, and serve with the sauce.

Note: For a thicker sauce, remove 1 tablespoon of sauce to a small bowl. Dissolve 1 teaspoon arrowroot powder in the sauce, then add back to the Instant Pot and whisk well. Select the Sauté setting and allow to cook for a few minutes, whisking often, until thickened.

The Easiest Indian Chicken Curry

20 Minutes or Less

Serves 4
Prep Time: 10 minutes
Cook Time: 8 minutes

Ingredients
1 tablespoon ghee
1½ large yellow onion, chopped
1 teaspoon salt
2 teaspoons garlic powder
2 teaspoons ground ginger
2 heaping teaspoons turmeric
¼ teaspoon cayenne powder
2 teaspoons paprika
2 teaspoons garam masala
1-15-oz can sweet potato puree
2 teaspoons red wine vinegar
2 teaspoons coconut aminos
2-14 oz. cans unsweetened coconut milk
2 lbs. boneless skinless chicken breasts or thighs

Directions
Select the Sauté setting and heat the ghee. Add the onion and cook until translucent, about 3-5 minutes. Add the salt, garlic powder, ground ginger, turmeric, cayenne, paprika, and garam masala, and sauté for 2 minutes. Add the sweet potato puree, red wine vinegar, coconut aminos, and unsweetened coconut milk and mix well. Add the chicken breasts or thighs and stir to coat in the sauce.

Press Cancel to reset the cooking method. Lock the lid and set the Pressure Release to Sealing. Select the Poultry setting and set the cooking time to 8 minutes at high pressure.

Once the timer goes off, let sit for at least 10 minutes; the pressure will release naturally. Then switch the Pressure Release to Venting to allow any last steam out.

Open the lid and taste, adding more salt and pepper if necessary. Break the chicken into smaller pieces but don't fully shred it. Serve with spiralized carrots or cauliflower rice.

Better-Than-Storebought Rotisserie Chicken

Kid-Friendly
7 Ingredients or Less

Serves 6
Prep Time: 15 minutes
Cook Time: 20 minutes

Ingredients
1 4-5 pound whole chicken
1 ½ teaspoons salt
Pepper to taste
2 teaspoons garlic powder
2 tablespoons olive oil
1 teaspoon thyme
1 lemon, juiced and zested
1 cup chicken broth

Directions
Pat the chicken dry with paper towels. In a small bowl, mix salt, pepper, garlic powder, olive oil, thyme, and lemon juice and zest. Rub the chicken with the herb oil.

Select the Sauté setting and add the chicken, back side down, to the pot. Sear for 6-7 minutes, until well browned, then flip and brown the breast side for another 6-7 minutes. Add the chicken broth and scrape up any browned bits stuck to the bottom of the pot.

Press Cancel to reset the cooking method. Lock the lid and set the Pressure Release to Sealing. Select the Poultry setting and set the cooking time to 20 minutes at high pressure.

Once the timer goes off, use a kitchen towel or oven mitts to protect your hand and move the Pressure Release knob to Venting to perform a quick pressure release.

Open the lid, and taste, adding more salt and pepper to the sauce if necessary. Transfer to a platter, carve, and serve warm.

Italian White Bean and Chicken Bowls

Kid-Friendly

Serves 4
Prep Time: 5 minutes
Cook Time: 40 minutes

Ingredients
2 cups dried white beans, such as great northern, cannellini, or chickpeas
1 yellow onion, chopped
3 cloves garlic, minced
½ teaspoon dried thyme
½ teaspoon dried oregano
1 teaspoon salt
Pepper to taste
4½ cups chicken or vegetable broth
1 lb. boneless chicken thighs or breasts, cut in 2-inch pieces
2 cups broccoli florets
Optional: Replace the thyme and oregano with 1 teaspoon of Lectin-Free Italian Seasoning (recipe found in the Seasonings chapter).
Optional: 1 lemon, juiced

Directions
In the Instant Pot, add the beans, onion, garlic, thyme, oregano, salt, pepper, and broth. Stir well and spread out the beans so that they're in an even layer and submerged in the broth. Place the chicken in an even layer over the beans.

Lock the lid and set the Pressure Release to Sealing. Select the Pressure Cook or Manual setting and set the cooking time to 40 minutes at high pressure.

Once the timer goes off, let sit for at least 10 minutes; the pressure will release naturally. Then switch the Pressure Release to Venting to allow any last steam out.

Open the Instant Pot and taste, adding more salt and pepper if needed. Select the Sauté setting and add the broccoli; allow to cook for 3-5 minutes, until tender. Spoon into bowls and serve warm, drizzled with olive oil, and if desired, a squeeze of fresh lemon juice.

Lectin-Free Instant Pot Seafood Recipes

Better-Than-Takeout Asian Salmon with Broccoli

Kid-Friendly
20 Minutes or Less

Serves 4
Prep Time: 5 minutes
Cook Time: 3 minutes

Ingredients:
2 cloves garlic, minced
¼ teaspoon crushed red pepper
½ teaspoon salt
Pepper to taste
3 tablespoons coconut aminos
1 cup chicken broth
2 cups broccoli florets
4 medium-sized salmon fillets
½ lime, juiced
1 tablespoon sesame oil

Directions
In a small bowl, combine half of the minced garlic, crushed red pepper, salt, pepper, and 2 tablespoons of the coconut aminos. Brush the sauce on the salmon fillets.

In the Instant Pot, add 1 cup of chicken broth and place the trivet in the bottom of the pot. Add the broccoli florets, and season to taste with salt and pepper. Arrange the salmon fillets on top of the broccoli.

Lock the lid and set the Pressure Release to Sealing. Select the Steam setting and set the cooking time to 3 minutes at high pressure. Meanwhile, in a small bowl, combine the lime juice, remaining minced garlic, remaining 1 tablespoon of coconut aminos, sesame oil, and salt and pepper to taste.

With a kitchen towel or oven mitts protecting your hand, move the Pressure Release knob to Venting to perform a quick pressure release.

Open the lid and taste, adding more salt and pepper if necessary. Serve the salmon and broccoli with the sesame oil sauce.

Easy Lemon Garlic Salmon with Cauliflower

Kid-Friendly
20 Minutes or Less
7 Ingredients or Less

Serves 4
Prep Time: 5 minutes
Cook Time: 3 minutes

Ingredients:
4 cloves garlic, minced
1 teaspoon salt, divided
Pepper to taste
2 tablespoons ghee, divided
2 tablespoons lemon juice, divided
1 medium onion, sliced
3 cups cauliflower in small florets
4 medium-sized salmon fillets

Directions
In a small bowl, combine half of the minced garlic, ½ teaspoon salt, pepper, and 1 tablespoon each of the ghee and lemon juice. Brush the lemon garlic sauce on the salmon fillets.

In the Instant Pot, add 1 cup of chicken broth and place the trivet in the bottom of the pot. Add the onions and cauliflower, and season lightly with salt and pepper. Arrange the salmon fillets on top of the onions and cauliflower.

Lock the lid and set the Pressure Release to Sealing. Select the Steam setting and set the cooking time to 3 minutes at high pressure. Meanwhile, in a small bowl, combine the remaining minced garlic, remaining 1 tablespoon of ghee, lemon juice, and salt and pepper to taste.

Once the timer has gone off and with a kitchen towel or oven mitts protecting your hand, move the Pressure Release knob to Venting to perform a quick pressure release.

Open the lid and taste, adding more salt and pepper if necessary. Serve the salmon and cauliflower with the lemon garlic sauce.

Light and Fresh Mediterranean Cod

20 Minutes or Less

Serves 4
Prep Time: 10 minutes
Cook Time: 6 minutes

Ingredients
1 tablespoon ghee
1 lemon, juiced
1 onion, sliced
½ teaspoon salt
½ teaspoon black pepper
1 teaspoon dried oregano
1-28 oz. can white beans (The Eden brand is pressure cooked before being canned, which greatly reduces the lectin content. It can be bought here: http://bit.ly/edenbeans)
1 cup chicken broth
2 tablespoons capers, drained, or 2 tablespoons Kalamata olives, chopped
6 cod fillets

Directions
Select the Sauté setting and heat the ghee. Add the remaining ingredients, except for the cod. Cook the sauce for 10 minutes. Place the cod fillets in the sauce and spoon sauce over each fillet.

Press Cancel to reset the cooking method. Lock the lid and set the Pressure Release to Sealing. Select the Steam setting and set the cooking time to 3 minutes at high pressure.

Once the timer has gone off and with a kitchen towel or oven mitts protecting your hand, move the Pressure Release knob to Venting to perform a quick pressure release.

Open the lid and taste the sauce, adding more salt and pepper if necessary. Serve the cod with the beans and Mediterranean sauce.

5-Minute Citrus Shrimp

Kid-Friendly
20 Minutes or Less
7 Ingredients or Less

Serves 4
Prep Time: 5 minutes
Cook Time: 1 minute

Ingredients
1 tablespoon ghee
4 garlic cloves, minced
½ cup orange juice (100% pure, no sugar added)
½ cup chicken broth
2 pounds of peeled and deveined raw shrimp
2 tablespoons lemon juice
½ teaspoon salt
Pepper to taste

Directions
Select the Sauté setting and heat the ghee. Add the garlic and cook until fragrant, 1-2 minutes. Add the orange juice and chicken broth.

Press Cancel to reset the cooking method, add the shrimp, and season with ½ teaspoon salt. Lock the lid and set the Pressure Release to Sealing. Select the Steam setting and set the cooking time to 1 minute at high pressure.

Once the timer has gone off and with a kitchen towel or oven mitts protecting your hand, move the Pressure Release knob to Venting to perform a quick pressure release.

Open the lid and stir in lemon juice and adjust salt and pepper to taste. Serve over cauliflower rice or mixed vegetables.

Lectin-Free Instant Pot Pork Recipes

Sunday Favorite Garlicky Pulled Pork

Kid-Friendly
7 Ingredients or Less

Serves 4
Prep Time: 5 minutes
Cook Time: 45 minutes

Ingredients
18 oz. pork tenderloin
1 teaspoon salt
½ teaspoon pepper
1 tablespoon olive oil
1 cup chicken broth
8 garlic cloves
2 sprigs of fresh thyme, or 2 teaspoons dried thyme
1 tablespoon fresh oregano, or 1 teaspoon dried oregano
Optional: 2 bay leaves

Directions
Season the pork loin with salt and pepper. Select the Sauté setting on the Instant Pot and heat the olive oil. Add the pork loin to the Instant Pot and sear on all sides until browned. Add the chicken broth, garlic, thyme, oregano, and if using, bay leaves.

Press Cancel to reset the cooking method. Lock the lid and set the Pressure Release to Sealing. Select the Meat/Stew setting and set the cooking time to 45 minutes at high pressure.

Once the timer goes off, let sit for at least 10 minutes; the pressure will release naturally. Then switch the Pressure Release to Venting to allow any last steam out.

Open the lid and taste, adding more salt and pepper if necessary. Shred the pork and serve over roasted brussels sprouts or spoon over vegetable fritters.

Mushroom Smothered Pork Chops

7 Ingredients or Less
20 Minutes or Less

Serves 4
Prep Time: 10 minutes
Cook Time: 15 minutes

Ingredients
4-½ inch thick bone-in pork chops
½ teaspoon paprika
½ teaspoon garlic powder
1 teaspoon salt
½ teaspoon ground black pepper
1 tablespoon ghee
1 onion, sliced
6 oz. mushrooms
½ cup chicken broth
Optional: 1 teaspoon arrowroot powder

Directions
Season the pork chops with paprika, garlic powder, salt and pepper. Select the Sauté setting on the Instant Pot and heat the ghee. Brown the chops on both sides then remove to a plate, working in batches of 2 chops at a time if necessary. Set aside the browned chops.

Add the onion and mushrooms and cook for about 3 minutes, stirring well. Add the chicken broth and nestle the pork chops back into the sauce.

Press Cancel to reset the cooking method. Lock the lid and set the Pressure Release to Sealing. Select the Meat/Stew setting and set the cooking time to 15 minutes at high pressure.

Once the timer has gone off and with a kitchen towel or oven mitts protecting your hand, move the Pressure Release knob to Venting to perform a quick pressure release.

Open the lid and taste, adding more salt and pepper if necessary. Remove the pork chops to a platter and allow to rest for 2-3 minutes before serving drizzled with the mushroom sauce.

Note: For a thicker sauce, remove 1 tablespoon of sauce to a small bowl. Dissolve 1 teaspoon arrowroot powder in the sauce, then add back to the Instant Pot and whisk well. Select the Sauté setting and allow to cook for a few minutes, whisking often, until thickened.

Artichoke and Lemon Pork Chops

Kid-Friendly
20 Minutes or Less

Serves 4
Prep Time: 10 minutes
Cook Time: 15 minutes

Ingredients
3 oz. bacon, diced
4-½ inch thick bone-in pork chops
2 teaspoons ground black pepper
1 shallot, minced
1 teaspoon lemon zest
3 garlic cloves, minced
1 teaspoon dried rosemary
1 cup chicken broth
1 9-oz package frozen artichoke heart quarters

Directions
Select the Sauté setting and add the bacon. Cook until it has rendered its fat and turned crispy, about 5 minutes. Transfer the bacon to a plate.

Season the pork chops with salt and pepper and add to the Instant Pot. Brown the chops on both sides then remove to a plate, working in batches of 2 chops at a time if necessary.

Add shallots to the pot and cook for 1 minute. Add lemon zest, garlic, and rosemary and cook until fragrant. Add the chicken broth, artichokes, and cooked bacon. Stir well then nestle the chops back into the sauce.

Press Cancel to reset the cooking method. Lock the lid and set the Pressure Release to Sealing. Select the Meat/Stew setting and set the cooking time to 15 minutes at high pressure.

Once the timer has gone off and with a kitchen towel or oven mitts protecting your hand, move the Pressure Release knob to Venting to perform a quick pressure release.

Open the lid and taste, adding salt and pepper if necessary. Serve the pork chops with the lemon artichoke sauce.

Cuban Pulled Pork, aka Ropa Vieja

Kid-Friendly
7 Ingredients or Less

Serve: 8
Prep Time: 5 minutes
Cook Time: 80 minutes

Ingredients
3 lbs. boneless pork shoulder, fat trimmed
6 cloves garlic
2/3 cup grapefruit juice (100% juice, no sugar added) (Grapefruit juice is lectin-free friendly when pressure cooked.)
½ tablespoon fresh oregano, or 1 teaspoon dried oregano
1 tablespoon cumin
1 lime, juiced
½ tablespoon salt
1 bay leaf
Optional for serving: lime wedges, cilantro, salsa, or hot sauce

Directions
Cut the pork shoulder into 4 evenly sized pieces. In a blender or food processor, combine the garlic, grapefruit juice, oregano, cumin, lime juice, and salt, and blend until combined. Place the pork shoulder pieces in the Instant Pot and rub with the sauce.

Lock the lid and set the Pressure Release to Sealing. Select the Meat/Stew setting and set the cooking time to 80 minutes at high pressure.

Once the timer goes off, let sit for at least 10 minutes; the pressure will release naturally. Then switch the Pressure Release to Venting to allow any last steam out.

Open the lid and taste, adding more salt and pepper if necessary. Remove the pork, shred, ladle sauce over it, and serve warm.

Note: For a thicker sauce, add the shredded pork back to the Instant Pot with the sauce. Select the Sauté setting and cook for 3-5 minutes until sauce has soaked into the pork.

5-Ingredient Kahlua Pork

Kid-Friendly
7 Ingredients or Less

Serves 8
Prep Time: 15 minutes
Cook Time: 80 minutes

Ingredients
3 lbs. boneless pork shoulder, fat trimmed
5 bacon slices
1 teaspoon salt
Pepper to taste
1 cup chicken or pork broth
6 cloves garlic
½ cup diced pineapple, canned (Pineapple is lectin-free friendly when pressure cooked.)
1 tablespoon liquid smoke

Directions
Select the Sauté setting and add the bacon. Cook until the bacon has rendered its fat and turned crispy, about 5 minutes. Transfer the bacon to a plate.

Cut the pork shoulder into 4 evenly sized pieces and season with salt and pepper. Add to the Instant Pot and sear on all sides until brown, about 4-6 minutes per side. Add 1 cup of chicken or pork broth, pineapple, garlic, and liquid smoke.

Press Cancel to reset the cooking method. Lock the lid and set the Pressure Release to Sealing. Select the Meat/Stew setting and set the cooking time to 80 minutes at high pressure.

Once the timer goes off, let sit for at least 10 minutes; the pressure will release naturally. Then switch the Pressure Release to Venting to allow any last steam out.

Open the lid and taste, adding more salt and pepper if necessary. Remove the pork, shred it, ladle sauce over it, and serve warm.

Note: For a thicker sauce, add the shredded pork back to the Instant Pot with the sauce. Select the Sauté setting and cook for 3-5 minutes until sauce has soaked into the pork.

Balsamic Glazed Pork Tenderloin

Kid-Friendly
7 Ingredients or Less
20 Minutes or Less

Serves 4
Prep Time: 15 minutes
Cook Time: 15 minutes

Ingredients

2 tablespoons ghee
1½ lb. boneless pork tenderloin
1 teaspoon salt
½ teaspoon black pepper
1 teaspoon garlic powder
1 large red onion, thinly sliced
1/3 cup balsamic vinegar
½ cup of chicken broth
Optional: 1 teaspoon arrowroot powder

Directions

Select the Sauté setting and heat the ghee. Season the pork loin on all sides with salt, pepper, and garlic powder. Add to the Instant Pot and sear on all sides until brown, about 3-4 minutes per side. Transfer the loin to a plate and set aside.

Add red onion to the Instant Pot and cook for 3-5 minutes, until translucent. Add balsamic vinegar and chicken broth, stir well, then nestle the pork loin back into the Instant Pot.

Press Cancel to reset the cooking method. Lock the lid and set the Pressure Release to Sealing. Select the Meat/Stew setting and set the cooking time to 15 minutes at high pressure.

Once the timer goes off, let sit for at least 10 minutes; the pressure will release naturally. Then switch the Pressure Release to Venting to allow any last steam out.

Open the lid and taste, adding more salt and pepper if necessary. Transfer the pork loin to a cutting board and allow to rest for 5 minutes. Slice and serve with the balsamic glaze.

Note: For a thicker glaze, remove 1 tablespoon of sauce to a small bowl. Dissolve 1 teaspoon arrowroot powder in the sauce, then add back to the Instant Pot and whisk well. Select the Sauté setting and allow to cook for a few minutes, whisking often, until thickened.

Cumin-Spiced Pulled Pork Carnitas

Kid-Friendly

Serves 6
Prep Time: 7 minutes
Cook Time: 40 minutes

Ingredients
3 lb. boneless pork shoulder, fat trimmed
2 tablespoons of olive oil
¾ cup chicken or pork broth
1 head butter lettuce
2 carrots, grated
2 limes, cut into wedges

For spice rub:
1 tablespoon cumin
1 tablespoon garlic powder
½ tablespoon salt
2 teaspoons oregano
1 teaspoon pepper
1 teaspoon coriander
½ teaspoon cayenne pepper

Directions
In a large bowl, combine the ingredients for the spice rub. Quarter the pork shoulder in 4 evenly sized pieces and rub all over with the cumin spice rub. Allow the pork to absorb the spice rub for 30 minutes or up to overnight in the refrigerator.

Select the Sauté setting and heat the olive oil. Add the pork shoulder to the Instant Pot and sear on all sides until brown, about 3-4 minutes per side. Add ¾ cup of chicken or pork broth and scrape up any browned bits at the bottom of the pot.

Press Cancel to reset the cooking method. Lock the lid and set the Pressure Release to Sealing. Select the Meat/Stew setting and set the cooking time to 40 minutes at high pressure.

Once the timer goes off, let sit for at least 10 minutes; the pressure will release naturally. Then switch the Pressure Release to Venting to allow any last steam out.

Remove the lid and taste the sauce; adjust seasoning if necessary. Shred the pork shoulder and serve in butter lettuce cups, topped with grated carrot and a squeeze of lime.

Optional: For a thicker sauce, add the shredded pork back to the Instant Pot with the sauce. Select the Sauté setting and cook for 3-5 minutes until sauce has soaked into the pork.

Lectin-Free Instant Pot Beef Recipes

Steak Fajita Stuffed Sweet Potatoes

Kid-Friendly

Prep Time: 15 Minutes
Cook Time: 20 minutes

Ingredients:
2 tablespoons olive oil, divided
1 ½ lbs. skirt steak, sliced
2 onions, sliced
¾ cup beef broth
4 medium sweet potatoes
Optional: lime wedges or guacamole for serving

For fajita seasoning:
1 tablespoon cumin
½ tablespoon chili powder
2 teaspoons garlic powder
¼ teaspoon cayenne pepper, or to taste
1 teaspoon dried oregano
1 teaspoon salt
½ teaspoon black pepper

Directions
In a small bowl, combine the chili powder, cumin, garlic powder, cayenne pepper, oregano, salt, and pepper. Pick the potatoes all over with a fork to allow steam to vent and wrap them in aluminum foil.

Select the Sauté setting on the Instant Pot and heat 1 tablespoon of the olive oil. Add half of the steak and sear on all sides. Remove to a plate and sear the second half of the steak. Remove to a plate again. Add the remaining 1 tablespoon of olive oil to the Instant Pot then add the onion. Sauté until cooked down and seared.

Add the beef broth to the Instant Pot and scrape up any browned bits from the bottom of the pot. Add the steak and spice mix and stir well. Place the trivet over the steak and onion. Place the foil-wrapped potatoes on top of the trivet. (It's okay if they get a bit wet with sauce.)

Press Cancel to reset the cooking method. Lock the lid and set the Pressure Release to Sealing. Select the Meat/Stew setting and set the cooking time to 20 minutes at high pressure.

Once the timer goes off, let sit for at least 10 minutes; the pressure will release naturally. Then switch the Pressure Release to Venting to allow any last steam out.

Remove the baked potatoes, slice open, and stuff with the steak and onion fajita mix. Serve with a squeeze of lime or guacamole.

Cajun Beef and Brussels Sprout Bowls

Kid-Friendly
20 Minutes or Less

Serves 4
Prep Time: 15 minutes
Cook Time: 5 minutes

Ingredients
2 tablespoons olive oil, divided
1½ lbs. beef stew meat, cubed
1 teaspoon salt
½ teaspoon pepper
1 teaspoon garlic powder
½ teaspoon paprika
½ teaspoon chili powder
¼ teaspoon cayenne pepper
½ teaspoon dried thyme
½ teaspoon dried oregano
1½ cups beef broth
1 large onion, quartered
1 lb. brussels sprouts, halved

Directions
Select the Sauté setting and heat 1 tablespoon of the olive oil. Add the beef and season with salt, pepper, garlic powder, paprika, chili powder, cayenne pepper, thyme, and oregano. Sear until well-browned on all sides, 5-7 minutes.

Add the beef broth to the Instant Pot and scrape up any browned bits from the bottom of the pot. Place trivet over the beef (it's okay if it's in the broth a bit). Layer the onion and brussels sprouts on top of the trivet and season lightly with salt and pepper.

Press Cancel to reset the cooking method. Lock the lid and set the Pressure Release to Sealing. Select the Manual or Pressure Cook setting and set the cooking time to 5 minutes at low pressure.

When the timer goes off, use a kitchen towel or oven mitts to protect your hand and move the Pressure Release knob to Venting to perform a quick pressure release.

Open the lid and taste, adding more salt and pepper if necessary. Spoon the brussels into individual bowls and served topped with the beef, either shredded or in chunks, and the sauce from the pot.

Red Wine Braised Beef Short Ribs

7 Ingredients or Less

Serves 5
Prep Time: 10 minutes
Cook Time: 45 minutes

Ingredients
4 pounds beef short ribs
½ tablespoon salt
1 tablespoon olive oil
1 medium onion, quartered
6 cloves garlic, minced
1 cup red wine
1 tablespoon red wine vinegar
1 cup beef broth
1 tablespoon fresh rosemary, or 1 ½ teaspoons dried rosemary

Directions
Season short ribs all over with salt. Select the Sauté setting on the Instant Pot and heat the olive oil. Brown the ribs on all sides, working in batches if necessary.

Add onion, garlic, red wine, red wine vinegar, beef broth, and rosemary to the Instant Pot, turning the ribs to coat them well.

Press Cancel to reset the cooking method. Lock the lid and set the Pressure Release to Sealing. Select the Meat/Stew setting and set the cooking time to 45 minutes at high pressure.

Once the timer goes off, let sit for at least 10 minutes; the pressure will release naturally. Then switch the Pressure Release to Venting to allow any last steam out.

Open the pot and taste the sauce; adjust the seasoning if necessary. Spoon the ribs and sauce over cauliflower rice or roasted brussels sprouts.

One-Pot Beef, Sweet Potato, and Kale Stew

Kid-Friendly

Serves 6
Prep Time: 10 minutes
Cook Time: 35 minutes

Ingredients
1 lb. beef stew meat, cubed
1 teaspoon salt
½ teaspoon pepper
1 tablespoon olive oil
1 medium onion, chopped
1 bunch kale, stemmed and chopped
2 medium sweet potatoes, cut in 2-inch pieces
4 medium carrots, sliced
2 cups beef broth
1 tablespoon red wine vinegar
1 teaspoon paprika
1 teaspoon onion powder
Optional: 1 teaspoon arrowroot powder

Directions
Season the meat with salt and pepper. Select the Sauté setting on the Instant Pot and heat the olive oil. Sear the meat until well-browned, 8-10 minutes. Add the onion, kale, sweet potatoes, carrots, beef broth, red wine vinegar, paprika, onion powder, and stir well.

Press Cancel to reset the cooking method. Lock the lid and set the Pressure Release to Sealing. Select the Meat/Stew setting and set the cooking time to 35 minutes at high pressure.

Once the timer goes off, let sit for at least 10 minutes; the pressure will release naturally. Then switch the Pressure Release to Venting to allow any last steam out.

Open the pot and taste the stew; adjust the seasoning if necessary.

Optional: For a thicker stew, ladle ¼ cup of the sauce into a small bowl and mix in 1 teaspoon arrowroot powder. Pour back into the Instant Pot, stir, and cook on the Sauté setting until thickened.

Burrito Bowl Lettuce Cups

Kid-Friendly

Serves 4
Prep Time: 10 minutes
Cook Time: 5 minutes

Ingredients
1 tablespoon olive oil
1 lb. ground beef
1 15-oz. can black beans (The Eden brand is pressure cooked before canning, or you can use 2 cups of homemade, pressure cooked black beans.)
1 cup beef broth
1 teaspoon salt
½ teaspoon black pepper
1 head butter lettuce, separated into lettuce cups
Optional: hot sauce, sliced green onions, guacamole, black olives, or other favorite burrito toppings

Spice mix:
½ tablespoon cumin
½ tablespoon chili powder
1 teaspoon garlic powder
1 teaspoon oregano
1 teaspoon onion powder
1 teaspoon salt
¼ teaspoon black pepper

Directions
Combine all spice mix ingredients in a small bowl. Select the Sauté setting on the Instant Pot and heat the olive oil. Add the ground beef and spice mix, and sear the meat until very well-browned, 8-10 minutes. Add the beans and beef broth and stir well.

Press Cancel to reset the cooking method. Lock the lid and set the Pressure Release to Sealing. Select the Manual or Pressure Cook setting and set the cooking time to 5 minutes at high pressure.

Once the timer goes off, let sit for at least 10 minutes; the pressure will release naturally. Then switch the Pressure Release to Venting to allow any last steam out.

Open the lid and taste, adding salt, pepper, or hot sauce to your taste. If you prefer the filling to be drier, select the Sauté setting and allow the liquid to cook down for 5-10 minutes. Serve the burrito filling scooped into lettuce cups with your favorite burrito toppings.

Note: For picky eaters, use less of the spice mix for a subtler flavor.

Simplest Beef Stroganoff

Kid-Friendly
20 Minutes or Less

Serves 4
Prep Time: 10 minutes
Cook Time: 18 minutes

Ingredients
1 tablespoon almond flour
1 teaspoon salt
¼ teaspoon pepper
1 lb. beef stew meat, cut into strips
1 tablespoon olive oil
1 onion, chopped
3 cloves garlic, minced
1 cup mushrooms, sliced
3 tablespoons red wine vinegar
1 cup beef broth

Directions
In a large bowl, mix the almond flour, salt, and pepper. Add the beef strips and toss to coat well. Select the Sauté setting on the Instant Pot and heat the olive oil. Shake any excess flour from the beef and sauté until well-browned. Add the remaining ingredients to the Instant Pot.

Press Cancel to reset the cooking method. Lock the lid and set the Pressure Release to Sealing. Select the Meat/Stew setting and set the cooking time to 18 minutes at medium pressure.

Once the timer goes off, let sit for at least 10 minutes; the pressure will release naturally. Then switch the Pressure Release to Venting to allow any last steam out.

Open the lid and taste, adding more salt and pepper if necessary. Serve with spiralized carrots or roasted sweet potatoes.

White Bean and Beef Pesto Bowls

Kid-Friendly

Serves 4
Prep Time: 5 minutes
Cook Time: 35 minutes

Ingredients
2 cups dried white beans, such as great northern, cannellini, or chickpeas
1 onion, chopped
3 cloves garlic, minced
1 teaspoon salt
¼ teaspoon pepper
5 cups beef broth
1 lb. ground beef
½ cup dairy-free pesto

For the dairy-free pesto:
1 cup fresh basil leaves (You can also use kale for a kale pesto.)
1 tablespoon pine nuts, walnuts, or almonds
1 large clove garlic
¼ cup extra virgin olive oil

Directions
In the Instant Pot, add the beans, onion, garlic, salt, pepper, and broth. Stir well and spread out the beans so that they're in an even layer and submerged in the broth. Add the ground beef in an even layer over the beans, breaking it up as you add it so it's in smaller pieces.

Lock the lid and set the Pressure Release to Sealing. Select the Pressure Cook or Manual setting and set the cooking time to 35 minutes at high pressure. While the beans and beef cook, combine all pesto ingredients in a food processor or blender.

Once the timer goes off, let sit for at least 10 minutes; the pressure will release naturally. Then switch the Pressure Release to Venting to allow any last steam out.

Open the Instant Pot and taste, adding more salt and pepper if needed. Stir in the pesto, spoon into bowls, and serve warm, drizzled with additional pesto, if desired.

Mexican Meatloaf with Sweet Potatoes

Kid-Friendly

Serves 4
Prep Time: 10 minutes
Cook Time: 20 minutes

Ingredients
1 cup beef broth
1 tablespoon ghee
1 teaspoon salt
½ teaspoon black pepper
4 medium sweet potatoes, in 1-inch pieces
1 pound ground beef
1 onion, finely chopped
1 egg

Spice mix:
½ tablespoon cumin
½ tablespoon chili powder
1 teaspoon garlic powder
1 teaspoon oregano
1 teaspoon onion powder
1 teaspoon salt
¼ teaspoon black pepper

Directions
In the bottom of the Instant Pot, stir the beef broth, ghee, salt, and pepper. Add the sweet potatoes and toss to coat. Place the Instant Pot trivet on top of the potatoes.

In a large bowl, combine the spice mix. Add the ground beef, onion, and egg, and mix until well incorporated. Set the meatloaf mix on a large piece of heavy duty foil or two stacked sheets of regular strength foil. Shape the meat into a loaf, then wrap the foil around it like a boat, leaving the top open. Gently place the foil-wrapped meatloaf on top of the trivet inside the Instant Pot.

Lock the lid and set the Pressure Release to Sealing. Select the Meat/Stew setting and set the cooking time to 20 minutes at high pressure.

Once the timer goes off, use a kitchen towel or oven mitts to protect your hand and move the Pressure Release knob to Venting to perform a quick pressure release.

Open the lid and taste, adding more salt and pepper if necessary. Brush the meatloaf with the broth in the pot, and if desired, place under the broiler for 1-2 minutes for a browner top. Serve alongside the potatoes and your favorite Mexican toppings.

Note: For picky eaters, use less of the spice mix for a subtler flavor.

Lectin-Free Instant Pot Vegetarian and Vegetable Side Recipes

Perfect Cauliflower Mash

Kid-Friendly
7 Ingredients or Less
20 Minutes or Less

Serves 4 as a side
Prep Time: 5 minutes
Cook Time: 5 minutes

Ingredients
1 large head cauliflower, cored and cut in large florets
1 cup chicken or vegetable broth
4 tablespoons ghee
½ tablespoon garlic powder
Salt to taste
Pepper to taste

Directions
Add the cauliflower and broth to the Instant Pot. Lock the lid and set the Pressure Release to Sealing. Select the Pressure Cook or Manual setting and set the cooking time to 5 minutes at high pressure.

Once the timer goes off, use a kitchen towel or oven mitts to protect your hand and move the Pressure Release knob to Venting to perform a quick pressure release.

Drain, reserving any excess broth, and return the cauliflower to the pot. With a potato masher, immersion blender, or fork, mash to your desired consistency, adding broth as needed for more moisture. Stir in the ghee and garlic powder, and add salt and pepper to taste.

Note: For more flavor, mix in fresh herbs such as thyme or rosemary before serving. You can also stir in a splash of unsweetened original almond milk for a creamier mash.

10-Minute Balsamic Roasted Beets

20 Minutes or Less
7 Ingredients or Less

Serves 6 as a side
Prep Time: 1 minute
Cook Time: 10 minutes

Ingredients
6 medium beets, unpeeled
3 tablespoons balsamic vinegar
2 tablespoons olive oil
Salt to taste
Pepper to taste

Directions
Wash the beets well and remove any leaves. Add 1 cup of water to the Instant Pot and place the trivet on top. Arrange the beets on the trivet.

Lock the lid and set the Pressure Release to Sealing. Select the Pressure Cook or Manual setting and set the cooking time to 10 minutes at high pressure.

Once the timer goes off, use a kitchen towel or oven mitts to protect your hand and move the Pressure Release knob to Venting to perform a quick pressure release.

Remove the beets, allow to cool, and peel. The skin should slip off easily. Slice the beets into rounds or chop them into bite-sized pieces. Dress them with the balsamic vinegar, olive oil, and salt and pepper to taste.

Serve immediately or allow to marinate for 30 minutes for more flavor.

Flavor Bomb Asian Brussels Sprouts

20 Minutes or Less

Serves 4
Prep Time: 5 minutes
Cook Time: 3 minutes

Ingredients
3 tablespoons coconut aminos
1 tablespoon rice wine vinegar
2 tablespoons sesame oil
2 teaspoons garlic powder
1 teaspoon onion powder
1 tablespoon paprika
¼ teaspoon cayenne pepper
1 teaspoon salt
1 tablespoon chopped almonds
2 lbs. Brussels sprouts, halved

Directions
In a small bowl, combine the coconut aminos, rice wine vinegar, sesame oil, garlic powder, onion powder, paprika, cayenne pepper, and salt. Set aside.

Select the Sauté setting and add the almonds. Stir constantly until toasted, watching them carefully so they don't burn. Press Cancel to turn off the Sauté setting then add the reserved sauce to the pot. Add the brussels sprouts and stir well to coat them in the sauce.

Lock the lid and set the Pressure Release to Sealing. Select the Pressure Cook or Manual setting and set the cooking time to 3 minutes at high pressure.

Once the timer goes off, use a kitchen towel or oven mitts to protect your hand and move the Pressure Release knob to Venting to perform a quick pressure release.

Open the lid and taste, adding salt and pepper to taste, if necessary. Serve warm over cauliflower rice or as a side for a protein.

Note: For spicier brussels sprouts, try doubling or tripling the quantity of cayenne pepper, or add a few tablespoons of your favorite lectin-free hot sauce.

Amazingly Adaptable Roasted Sweet Potatoes

Kid-Friendly
7 Ingredients or Less
20 Minutes or Less

Serves 4
Prep Time: 5 minutes
Cook Time: 7 minutes

Ingredients
¼ cup olive oil or ghee
4 medium sweet potatoes, peeled or unpeeled, in 1-inch pieces
1 teaspoon garlic powder
1 teaspoon sea salt
¼ teaspoon pepper
1 cup chicken or vegetable broth

Directions
Select the Sauté setting on the Instant Pot and heat the olive oil or ghee. Add the sweet potatoes, salt, pepper, and garlic powder to the pot and sauté for 5 minutes, stirring constantly. Add the broth and stir well.

Press Cancel to reset the cooking method. Lock the lid and set the Pressure Release to Sealing. Select the Pressure Cook or Manual setting and set the cooking time to 7 minutes at high pressure.

Once the timer goes off, use a kitchen towel or oven mitts to protect your hand and move the Pressure Release knob to Venting to perform a quick pressure release.

Open the lid and taste, adding salt and pepper to taste, if necessary. Serve warm over a salad or as a side for chicken or another protein.

Note: This recipe can be adapted many ways, according to your family's tastes. Try adding a favorite spice mix, curry powder, or cayenne pepper before pressure cooking, fresh herbs like rosemary and thyme after cooking, or a drizzle of truffle oil before serving.

Simplest Brothy Beans

Kid-Friendly
7 Ingredients or Less

Serves 4
Prep Time: 5 minutes
Cook Time: 35 minutes

Ingredients
1 lb. dried white beans, such as great northern, cannellini, or chickpeas
1 yellow onion, quartered
2 celery stalks, cut in half
2 carrots, peeled and cut in half
8 cups water
Salt to taste
Freshly ground pepper to taste
Extra virgin olive oil to taste
Optional: 1 lemon, juiced

Directions
In the Instant Pot, add the beans, onion, celery, carrots, water, and 1 teaspoon of salt. Lock the lid and set the Pressure Release to Sealing. Select the Pressure Cook or Manual setting and set the cooking time to 35 minutes at high pressure.

Once the timer goes off, let sit for at least 10 minutes; the pressure will release naturally. Then switch the Pressure Release to Venting to allow any last steam out.

Open the Instant Pot and season beans generously with salt and pepper, tasting the broth as you add seasoning until it's to your taste. Serve warm, drizzled with olive oil, and if desired, a squeeze of fresh lemon juice.

Southern Stewed Greens

7 Ingredients or Less
20 Minutes or Less

Serves 4 as a side
Prep Time: 10 minutes
Cook Time: 5 minutes

Ingredients
¼ lb. bacon, in 1-inch pieces (omit to make this dish vegetarian)
5 cloves garlic, roughly chopped
2 large bunches kale, collard greens, or chard, de-stemmed and roughly chopped
3/4 cup chicken or vegetable broth
Salt to taste
Pepper to taste
Optional: 1 tablespoon apple cider vinegar

Directions
Select the Sauté setting and add the bacon, cooking until it has rendered its fat and crisped up, 5-7 minutes. Add the garlic and cook, stirring constantly, for 1 minute. Add the greens, broth, and salt and pepper to taste. You may need to add the greens in batches, stir, and allow to wilt slightly until it all fits in the pot.

Press Cancel to reset the cooking method. Lock the lid and set the Pressure Release to Sealing. Select the Pressure Cook or Manual setting and set the cooking time to 5 minutes at high pressure.

Once the timer goes off, use a kitchen towel or oven mitts to protect your hand and move the Pressure Release knob to Venting to perform a quick pressure release.

Open the lid, taste, and add more salt and pepper if necessary. If desired, stir in 1 tablespoon of apple cider vinegar to add brightness to the dish. Serve warm.

Garlicky Mashed Sweet Potatoes

Kid-Friendly
7 Ingredients or Less
20 Minutes or Less

Serves 4
Prep Time: 5 minutes
Cook Time: 8 minutes

Ingredients
4 medium sweet potatoes, peeled and cut into 1-inch chunks
1 cup vegetable broth
6 cloves garlic, peeled and halved
½ cup unsweetened original almond milk
½ tablespoon garlic powder
3 tablespoons ghee
Salt to taste
Pepper to taste
Optional: 1 tablespoon chopped parsley for serving

Directions
In the Instant Pot, add the sweet potatoes, broth, and garlic. Lock the lid and set the Pressure Release to Sealing. Select the Pressure Cook or Manual setting and set the cooking time to 8 minutes at high pressure.

Once the timer goes off, use a kitchen towel or oven mitts to protect your hand and move the Pressure Release knob to Venting to perform a quick pressure release.

Open the Instant Pot and mash the potatoes using a potato masher, immersion blender, or fork. Stir in the almond milk, garlic powder, and ghee, and add salt and pepper to taste.

Serve warm and sprinkle with fresh parsley, if desired.

Balsamic and Garlic Stewed Kale

20 Minutes or Less
7 Ingredients or Less

Serves 4 as a side
Prep Time: 5 minutes
Cook Time: 4 minutes

Ingredients
1 tablespoon olive oil
5 cloves garlic, roughly chopped
2 large bunches kale, de-stemmed and roughly chopped
1 cup chicken broth
Salt to taste
Pepper to taste
3 tablespoons balsamic vinegar

Directions
Select the Sauté setting and heat the olive oil. Add the garlic and cook, stirring constantly, until fragrant, 3-5 minutes. Add the kale, broth, and salt and pepper to taste.

Press Cancel to reset the cooking method. Lock the lid and set the Pressure Release to Sealing. Select the Pressure Cook or Manual setting and set the cooking time to 4 minutes at high pressure.

Once the timer goes off, use a kitchen towel or oven mitts to protect your hand and move the Pressure Release knob to Venting to perform a quick pressure release.

Open the lid and add the balsamic vinegar. Taste and add more salt and pepper if necessary. Serve warm.

Easiest Baked Sweet Potatoes

Kid-Friendly
7 Ingredients or Less

Serves 4
Prep Time: 1 minute
Cook Time: 20 minutes

Ingredients
4 medium sweet potatoes

Directions
Place the Instant Pot trivet inside the pot. Prick the potatoes all over with a fork to allow them to vent. Arrange potatoes in one layer on top of the trivet and add 1 cup of water to the pot.

Lock the lid and set the Pressure Release to Sealing. Select the Steam setting and set the cooking time to 20 minutes at high pressure.

Once the timer goes off, let sit for at least 10 minutes; the pressure will release naturally. Then switch the Pressure Release to Venting to allow any last steam out.

Carefully remove the hot potatoes and serve warm.

Lectin-Free Sauces and Seasonings

Lectin-Free Lemon Pepper Seasoning

Kid-Friendly
7 Ingredients or Less
20 Minutes or Less

Prep Time: 5 Minutes
Cook Time: 0 minutes

Ingredients
6 lemons, zested
2 teaspoons garlic powder
1 tablespoon freshly cracked black pepper
2 teaspoons salt

In a small bowl, combine all ingredients. Store in a tight-sealing container in the refrigerator and use on chicken, fish, vegetables, and more.

Lectin-Free Taco Seasoning

Kid-Friendly
7 Ingredients or Less
20 Minutes or Less

Prep Time: 2 Minutes
Cook Time: 0 minutes

Ingredients
2 tablespoons chili powder
1½ tablespoons ground cumin
2 teaspoons garlic powder
¼ teaspoon cayenne pepper, or to taste
1 teaspoon dried oregano
2 teaspoons salt
1 teaspoon black pepper

In a small bowl, combine all ingredients. Store in a tight-sealing container at room temperature and use on chicken, fish, meat, sweet potatoes, vegetables, and more.

Lectin-Free Italian Seasoning

Kid-Friendly
7 Ingredients or Less
20 Minutes or Less

Prep Time: 2 Minutes
Cook Time: 0 minutes

Ingredients
1 tablespoon garlic powder
½ tablespoon dried oregano
1 teaspoon dried basil
1 teaspoon dried thyme
1 teaspoon salt
1 teaspoon black pepper

In a small bowl, combine all ingredients. Store in a tight-sealing container at room temperature and use on chicken, fish, meat, sweet potatoes, vegetables, and more.

You can also make a delicious Italian dressing by adding olive oil and apple cider vinegar to this seasoning and shaking well. This makes a healthy, lectin-free, sugar-free Italian dressing that can be used to marinate chicken, fish, and pork or can be drizzled over roasted vegetables.

Lectin-Free Indian Spice Mix

Kid-Friendly
7 Ingredients or Less
20 Minutes or Less

Prep Time: 2 Minutes
Cook Time: 0 minutes

Ingredients
2 tablespoons curry powder
2 tablespoons cumin
2 teaspoons turmeric
2 teaspoons ground coriander
1 teaspoon ground ginger
½ teaspoon cinnamon

In a small bowl, combine all ingredients. Store in a tight-sealing container at room temperature and use on in curries or on chicken, fish, meat, sweet potatoes, vegetables, and more.

Cooking Times for the Instant Pot Electric Pressure Cooker

The Instant Pot and other electric pressure cookers are miracle workers for transforming lectin-bomb foods into lectin-free foods. By pressure cooking foods like grains, beans, squash, tomatoes, and more, you can drastically reduce the quantity of harmful lectins found in them.

However, since each phase of a lectin-free diet is different, and each person's body chemistry is different, I've included the suggested cooking times for a wide range of foods here. You can check the lectin-level of nearly any food with a quick online search, and always consult your doctor before reintegrating new foods after doing an elimination diet like a lectin-free diet.

This list will also prove useful for feeding family members who aren't going lectin-free or aren't trying to reduce the lectins in their diet. With an electric pressure cooker like the Instant Pot, you can cook up nearly a week's worth of rice, quinoa, black beans, lentils, or other meal-building staples in just a few minutes. That way, your family can still eat the things they enjoy, even while you opt out (from both eating them *and* cooking them nightly!).

Keep these times handy for anytime you need a simple staple ingredient done quickly.

A note on cooking beans and other legumes in the Instant Pot:
Dried beans will double in volume after cooking, so never fill your electric pressure cooker more than halfway and be sure to fully cover the beans with liquid.

Dried Beans, Legumes, and Lentils	DRY Cooking Time (minutes)	SOAKED Cooking Time (minutes)
Black beans	20 – 25	6 – 8
Black-eyed peas	10 – 15	4 – 5
Chickpeas (chickpeas, garbanzo beans)	35 – 40	10 – 15
Cannellini beans	30 – 35	8 – 10
Great Northern beans	25 – 30	8 – 10
Kidney beans, red	25 – 30	8 – 10
Kidney beans, white / Cannellini	30 – 35	8 – 10
Lentils, green	10 – 12	n/a

Lentils, brown	10 – 12	n/a
Lentils, red, split	5 – 6	n/a
Lentils, yellow, split (moong dal)	18 – 20	n/a
Lima beans	12 – 14	8 – 10
Navy beans	20 – 25	7 – 8
Pinto beans	25 – 30	8 – 10
Peas	6 – 10	n/a

Meat	Cooking Time (mins)
Beef, stew meat	20 / 450 gm / 1 lb
Beef, meatballs	8-10 / 450 gm / 1 lb
Beef (pot roast, steak, rump, round, chuck, blade or brisket), small pieces	15 / 450 gm / 1 lb
Beef (pot roast, steak, rump, round, chuck, blade or brisket), large pieces	20 / 450 gm / 1 lb
Beef, ribs	20 – 25
Beef, shanks	25 – 30
Chicken, breasts (boneless)	6 – 8
Chicken, whole 2-2.5 Kg	8 / 450 gm / 1 lb
Chicken, cut with bones	10 – 15
Chicken, bone stock	40 – 45
Ham, slices	9 – 12
Ham, picnic shoulder	8 / 450 gm / 1 lb

Lamb, cubes	10 – 15
Lamb, stew meat	12 – 15
Lamb, leg	15 / 450 gm / 1 lb
Pork, loin roast	20 / 450 gm / 1 lb
Pork, butt roast	15 / 450 gm / 1 lb
Pork, ribs	15 – 20
Turkey, breast (boneless)	7 – 9
Turkey, breast (whole)	20 – 25
Turkey, drumsticks (leg)	15 – 20
Veal, chops	5 – 8
Veal, roast	12 / 450 gm / 1 lb

Guidelines for Buying Organic Produce and Whole Foods

Buying organic can be expensive, but we all want to feed our families the healthiest and safest fruits and vegetables. That's where the Dirty Dozen and Clean Fifteen come in.

Each year, the Environmental Working Group issues its Shopper's Guide to Pesticides in Produce, which ranks the pesticide contamination of popular fruits and vegetables. Rankings are based on data from more than 35,200 samples which are tested each year by the U.S. Department of Agriculture and the Food and Drug Administration.

The top 15 types of produce that have the least amount of pesticide residue are known as the Clean Fifteen, while the top 12 most contaminated fruits and vegetables are called the Dirty Dozen.

By knowing which fruits and vegetables contain more pesticides and which contain less, you can make more informed choices and stretch your grocery dollar further.

The Dirty Dozen

When possible, buy these organic. To be lectin-free compliant, fruit should only be eaten when in season.

1. Strawberries
2. Spinach
3. Nectarines
4. Apples
5. Peaches
6. Pears
7. Cherries
8. Grapes
9. Celery
10. Tomatoes *lectin-free only when peeled and seeded
11. Sweet bell peppers *lectin-free only when peeled and seeded
12. Potatoes *swap for sweet potatoes when going lectin-free

The Clean Fifteen

These do not need to be bought organic. To be lectin-free compliant, fruit should only be eaten when in season.

1. Sweet Corn
2. Avocados
3. Pineapples
4. Cabbage
5. Onions
6. Sweet peas *Peas are actually legumes, so they should only be eaten if pressure cooked.
7. Papayas
8. Asparagus

9. Mangos
10. Eggplant *not lectin-free
11. Honeydew Melon
12. Kiwi
13. Cantaloupe
14. Cauliflower
15. Grapefruit

Metric Conversion Charts

If you use metric measurements in your cooking, use these handy charts to convert the recipes in this book to work in your kitchen. You can also find a free and easy-to-use metric conversion calculator at: https://www.convert-me.com/en/convert/cooking or with a quick online search.

1/4 tsp	= 1 ml		
1/2 tsp	= 2 ml		
1 tsp	= 5 ml		
3 tsp	= 1 tbl	= 1/2 fl oz	= 15 ml
2 tbls	= 1/8 cup	= 1 fl oz	= 30 ml
4 tbls	= 1/4 cup	= 2 fl oz	= 60 ml
5 1/3 tbls	= 1/3 cup	= 3 fl oz	= 80 ml
8 tbls	= 1/2 cup	= 4 fl oz	= 120 ml
10 2/3	= 2/3 cup	= 5 fl oz	= 160 ml
12 tbls	= 3/4 cup	= 6 fl oz	= 180 ml
16 tbls	= 1 cup	= 8 fl oz	= 240 ml
1 pt	= 2 cups	= 16 fl oz	= 480 ml
1 qt	= 4 cups	= 32 fl oz	= 960 ml
		33 fl oz	= 1000 ml = 1 l

Freeze Water	32° F	0° C	
Room Temp.	68° F	20° C	
Boil Water	212° F	100° C	
Bake	325° F	160° C	3
	350° F	180° C	4
	375° F	190° C	5
	400° F	200° C	6
	425° F	220° C	7
	450° F	230° C	8

Helpful Resources

If you'd like to learn more about the lectin-free diet and the Instant Pot electric pressure cooker, I highly recommend these books:

The Essential Instant Pot Cookbook: Fresh and Foolproof Recipes for Your Electric Pressure Cooker by Coco Morante [add aff links]

Dinner in an Instant: 75 Modern Recipes for Your Pressure Cooker, Multicooker, and Instant Pot by Melissa Clark

The Plant Paradox: The Hidden Dangers in "Healthy" Foods That Cause Weight Gain and Disease by Dr. Steven R. Gundry

The Plant Paradox Cookbook: 100 Delicious Recipes to Help You Lose Weight, Heal Your Gut, and Live Lectin-Free by Dr. Steven R. Gundry

Did you find these recipes helpful?

If so, would you consider paying it forward by leaving a review on Amazon?

A review is the best way to help me spread the word about this book, and hopefully it will help the next person find their way to healthier, easier Lectin-Free Instant Pot meals, too!

To leave a review:

Google search "lectin free cookbook Virginia Campbell" and click the first Amazon link. Or, copy this URL into your browser: http://bit.ly/lectinreview.

This should take you to the Amazon book page, where you can leave a review.

Thank you so much!

Gift a book = give a meal!

We believe everybody deserves a warm, healthy meal to come home to. That's why we've committed to donating one meal to a family in need through Feeding America for each copy sold of this book. So just by purchasing a copy of this book, you've helped feed a neighbor in need—thank you so much for that.

To spread the love even more, you can also gift a copy of this book to a friend. They'll love you for it, and you'll be making a difference in another family's life!

To gift a book:

Google search "lectin free cookbook Virginia Campbell" and click the first Amazon link.

Or, type this URL into your browser: http://bit.ly/lectinreview.

This should take you to the book page, where on the right, you'll see a button that says "Give as a Gift."

Happy gifting!

CPSIA information can be obtained
at www.ICGtesting.com
Printed in the USA
LVHW06s0523161018
593411LV00003BA/7/P